BUDDHISM AND DRUGS

BRIAN TAYLOR

道
UNIVERSAL OCTOPUS

Also available:

What is Buddhism?
The Living Waters of Buddhism
The Five Buddhist Precepts
Basic Buddhist Meditation
Basic Buddhism for a World in Trouble
Dependent Origination
The Ten Fetters (Saŋyojana)
Buddhist Pali Chants (with English Translations)
The Five Nivāraṇas
(Buddha's Teaching of the Five Hindrances)

Published by Universal Octopus 2017
www.universaloctopus.com

ISBN 978-1-9999063-1-3

CONTENTS

INTRODUCTION

Appamādo amatapadaṃ
pamādo maccuno padaṃ
appamattā na mīyanti
ye pamattā yathā matā.

Vigilance is the state of deathlessness.
Negligence is the state of death.
The Vigilant do not die.
The Negligent are as if dead already.

(*Dhammapada Verse 21*)

Amatapadaṃ means Deathlessness.

This is the goal of Buddhism. Nibbāna. No-one normally wants to die. The Path laid down by the Buddha is the *Path to the Deathless*.

The two key words are **appamādo** and **amatapadaṃ**.

Appamādo is carefulness; vigilance. This is fundamental to the practice of Buddhism. It indicates how everything is to be <u>done</u>. With vigilance. The original meaning of "*vigil*" is "*the awakened state.*"

Vigilance is a fundamental mental virtue. Without it, you make mistakes. You cannot achieve your goal.

A tennis player knows this. His concentration wavers? He loses the point.

But only one point!

Think of a racing driver. His concentration wavers?

He hits a wall?

Yes, but he's got a safety belt!

Think of Blondin crossing Niagara

on a tightrope.

Blondin walks the tightrope
over Niagara,
forwards, backwards,
blindfolded, on a bicycle,
to distant applause
among crashing waters.

Ten times, twenty, fifty....

One step missed
answers the first step taken
onto the swaying rope.

Then, everything is,
as it has always been;
jagged rocks and thundering waters.

Into the silence
where yesterday's applause
cannot reach.

Vigilance doesn't necessarily come naturally. It has to be developed.

Without it, we cannot proceed on our path towards enlightenment, which is actually the state of being awake.

If we are negligent, we cannot find the energy to focus on purifying our minds.

So, vigilance is the path to deathlessness. Only with vigilance can we find our way to the final goal, Nirvana, the deathless state.

Negligence on the other hand is the way to the repeated cycles of birth and death.

The Vigilant are able to escape the cycle of rebirths. The Negligent cannot escape. They are unaware and might as well be dead already.

It is **pamādo**, a mental state of negligence and carelessness, which is the target of the Fifth Buddhist Precept.

Intoxicating drinks and drugs fuel this mental state via the body. This leads humans to more rather than less suffering.

Vigilance is the state of deathlessness.
Negligence is the state of death.
The Vigilant do not die.
The Negligent are as if dead already.

Appamādo amatapadaṃ
pamādo maccuno padaṃ
appamattā na mīyanti
ye pamattā yathā matā.

BUDDHA

The Founder of Buddhism was a young prince, named Siddhartha, who was heir-presumptive to the kingdom of the Sakyan Clan in Northern India. Married at sixteen, he had a son, was in good health and lived the life that only the prosperous and well-endowed can live in any age.

In his twenties, he began to see through this veil of prosperity. He became aware of sickness, old age and death which are the unsatisfactory characteristics of human life. He also became aware that there were many ascetics, who had left home to search for a solution to this unsatisfactoriness.

At the age of 29, he, too, renounced everything and left palace, home and family to follow their example. He visited the famous teachers of his time and practised with them. He achieved all that they had. They invited him to join them as a joint teacher. But he was still not satisfied with what he had achieved.

He tried extreme asceticism in an effort to liberate the mind by torturing the body. Still no success.

Finally, after a reputed 49 days of meditation, and at the age of 35, he is said to have found the answers to all his questions. For the remainder of his eighty years he taught what he had attained and how to attain it.

During this time, he was known as Buddha, The Awakened One[1].

---

[1] Awakened One: *See Notes page 21*

Awakened from what?

From the dream of Ignorance that prevents men from seeing the obvious Truth.

What is this obvious Truth?

The Truth that all the experiences of Life, good and bad, noble and ignoble, occur within the framework of birth and death. All living beings must pass through this framework. Here they experience sickness, old age and death. And they don't get what they want.

Or if they do get what they want, they find that it doesn't last. Or else they discover that they no longer want it.

Is that all?

No. He also discovered that everything operates by way of cause and effect. If this, then that. And, of the greatest practical importance; if <u>not</u> this then <u>not</u> that. If I drop my glass onto a slate floor, it will break. If I break the Law of the land, I will be punished. If I dive off a skyscraper, I will break my neck.

In each case; if I don't, it won't happen.

Everyone knows this to a degree. The Awakened One applied it to everything.

If no birth, no death.

So what?

So, none of the sufferings and unsatisfactory experiences which can occur between birth and death.

Contemporary Greek philosophy had discovered this too. A little later, Sophocles was quoting, *"Not to be born is best"*. However, the Greeks got no further than this:

"If you are born, make the best of it".

But this is ambiguous. It can mean: lead a good and useful life. Or it can mean: indulge yourself while you can. Latin: *carpe diem.*

So why are we born?

Because there is an urge to become. Buddha says that without the mental urge to be born as a separate being, there can be no death as a separate being. To avoid death, don't get born.

No life and death as a separate being? Does that mean nothingness? Extinction?

No. Underlying and concealed behind all the paraphernalia of becoming, of being born and having to die, is an eternal, unmoving state. Perfect peace and happiness. This he called Nibbāna.

Nibbānam paranam sukham.
Nibbāna is the Highest Happiness.

But how do you not get born?

Live the right life. Make the right decisions. You will end up not being born again. In addition, the remainder of your present life will become progressively happier and more peaceful as well!

And what are these "right decisions"?

The Buddha makes it simple.

If you don't want any more suffering, begin by not causing suffering to yourself and others.

This is where the Five Precepts fit in. These are mental intentions to avoid causing suffering in key areas of a human life.

Why mental?

Because, the Buddha teaches, Mind comes first. If you want to change things and take charge of your life or destiny, you start with your own mind.

Buddhism identifies five areas in which we can stop doing things that cause suffering. It structures them as personal commitments, which a true Buddhist is supposed to make.

They are commitments not to cause suffering to self and others. The underlying basic Ethic is:

Don't do to other living beings what you (a living being) would not want done to you.

   You don't want to be killed, so don't kill.
   You don't want to be robbed, so don't steal.
   You don't want to be sexually abused, so don't be a paedophile.
   You don't want to be lied to, so speak the truth.

You don't want to be the victim of your own carelessness (crashing your car) or make others the victim of your carelessness (hitting someone else with your car), so don't drive when you are drunk or drugged.

In the Buddha's teaching, these commitments are codified in the form of the following precepts:

1. *I undertake to observe the precept to abstain from killing living beings.*

2. *I undertake to observe the precept to abstain from taking things not given.*

3. *I undertake to observe the precept to abstain from misuse of the senses[2].*

4. *I undertake to observe the precept to abstain from false speech.*

5. *I undertake to observe the precept to abstain from drinks and drugs causing heedlessness.*

The gateway to the Buddhist Path is these Five Precepts. Anyone who cannot understand these precepts and willingly put them into practice cannot be said to be a practising Buddhist. Not even if he wears a yellow robe. He will be a "Buddhist" in name only.

Nor can he gain the fruit of Buddhism – Nibbāna.

It is obvious that if one sticks to the spirit and letter of these precepts, one will eliminate serious ways in which one is a threat to others and oneself.

By doing this, one takes a stand against suffering and one comes to see it all the more clearly in daily life.

The fact that one articulates them in this way re-enforces the vigilance, **appamādo,** which is needed to actually put them into practice and reap the benefit.

With this, the Path to Peace begins.

---

[2] Misuse of the Senses: *See Notes pages 21-22*

BUDDHISM AND DRUGS

T he emphasis in Buddhism is always on identifying the *cause* of suffering.

So it works from the inside out. Although it acknowledges all those things in the world outside which make us suffer, it does not start with them.

With drugs, this involves looking not at what is done to one but what one *does*. It starts by trying to eliminate all those things that one does, which *cause* suffering to oneself and others.

After all, most of us don't have much control over what goes on in the world outside. But we can control what we ourselves do or don't do. So we start with that.

With drugs, this is addressed in the Fifth Precept:

Surā meraya majja pamādaṭṭhānā veramaṇī sikkhāpadaṃ samādiyāmi.

Surā - an intoxicating liquor.
Meraya - a fermented liquor.
Majja - an intoxicant.
Pamāda - carelessness, negligence.
māda - intoxication, cognate with "mad" in English, from a shared Indo-European root.
ṭhāna - cause.

I undertake to observe the precept to refrain from intoxicating drinks and drugs which cause carelessness or negligence.

Sura, meraya and **majja** are kinds of alcoholic, fermented and distilled intoxicating drinks. But they are not forbidden because they are <u>drinks</u>. But because they are intoxicants. Intoxicants cause carelessness. It is obvious that substances other than drinks can come under this heading.

In the present day, intoxicating drugs, which cause carelessness, are a world-wide and major problem.

They have always been a problem for the individual (suffering for self) but now they are increasingly a problem because they cause suffering for others with whom one associates or for whom one is responsible.

In the modern world, the Fifth Precept targets substances like alcohol and narcotics, and stimulants and hallucinogens like amphetamines and LSD.

Why does a Buddhist undertake to abstain from these things?

Because they lead to carelessness, the opposite of vigilance.

Carelessness leads to mistakes. These have consequences which are a source of regret and suffering.

Modern societies are full of broken lives and human disasters that are the results of alcohol and drug abuse. Crime, road accidents, poverty, broken homes, violence, physical illness, mental illness and misery.

Buddhism teaches Karma, cause and effect. If this, then that. If not this, then not that. In dealing with things, Buddhism seeks out the causes. If you change the cause, the effect changes automatically.

If, on the other hand, you merely remove the effects and leave the cause untouched, that cause will produce more effects of the same kind. You cut the weeds. They grow again. If you want to get rid of them altogether, you have to dig out their roots.

So why do people make themselves the victims of intoxicating substances in the first place?

When one first experiments with alcohol and drugs, one may like what they do to body and mind.

One may feel exhilarated, excited, ecstatic even. There may be a feeling of well-being or greater self-confidence.

They may help to overcome, or even temporarily disperse altogether, thoughts or memories that are painful or worrying. They may provide relief from excessive physical pain.

In short, they make one feel better. They can even make one temporarily more aware.

But in the long term they turn out to be more like the bait, which ensnares a fish.

Inside the bait is a hook!

The desirable experiences fade. One needs to take more to get less. Two pints instead of one. Two pills. Two joints. The doses increase. The pleasure does not.

Stronger drugs are needed. Cocaine and opium replace cannabis. Heroin replaces cocaine. LSD replaces amphetamines. Whisky and vodka replace beer.

Heightened awareness is replaced by torpor.

The decrease in pleasure is accompanied by a corresponding increase in the negative effects.

The body becomes increasingly unwell with nausea, pains in the joints and muscles, headaches, fever, loss of appetite, difficulty sleeping, a serious weakening of the immune system.

Mentally, there are mood swings from elation to depression, an inability to concentrate, paranoia and loss of memory.

At this stage one is drinking and taking drugs not for pleasure, but in order to get a momentary respite from suffering. One is seriously ill.

Inevitably, one's relationships suffer. One finds it difficult to keep a job. Money becomes a serious problem because as one finds it harder to earn it, the costs of buying alcohol or drugs in the quantities needed for even temporary relief escalate. It is a bleak picture.

Rehabilitation is difficult.

Withdrawal symptoms are severe. One hundred percent recovery is uncommon. Often the optimum result is "containment". This means that the patient is kept relatively stable by prescribed "safe" drugs.

"Relatively stable" does not mean he is happy, healthy and enjoying a good life. It means that, while on the medication (which will always have its own side-effects), he may be less of a social problem to others.

Quite commonly, there is a relapse. A return to drinking and drug-taking. The destructive cycle repeats itself.

Mind and body are weakened, and serious illness and consequent death are often the result.

It is not only the individual who is affected. The effects on his or her family are devastating. For children, to grow up in a family where there is drink or drug abuse is a terrible start to life.

Of course, prevention is better than cure. But it seems clear that the drug education programmes in schools aren't entirely successful.

glasses are for people with bad eyes.

Brian

Their efforts are not helped by the entertainment artists who target the young. They are often alcoholics and drug takers themselves and contribute to a drug culture as role models.

The sad fact is that the entertainment industry makes a lot of money and is very powerful.

At the present time, it is not possible for a democratic government to confront all of the unwholesome propaganda which targets the young and vulnerable.

Assuming that it had the will to do so.

Certainly, in the western democracies, punitive legislation has not worked.

When I ask you nicely, you don't do it.

If a water pipe is leaking, the result is water all over the place. If you spend your time mopping up the water with a cloth, you will be at it for a long time. To solve the problem you must find the cause of the leak and mend it.

With Buddhism, this simple logical approach is applied to everything.

Primarily, it is applied to the fact of suffering. If you wish to escape from suffering you must remove the cause of suffering. If you want to avoid the consequences of alcohol or drug addiction, leave alcohol and drugs alone.

SMOKAJOINTA

They say it's bad for for you, don't you?

Brian

Drugs are substances which lead men to carelessness with their own bodies, which become sick and degenerate and with their minds. Their judgement becomes impaired They make mistakes in handling their personal affairs, in their work, in their driving, in their relationships with others. If they have families and dependents, these too are affected by the errors of judgement resulting from this carelessness.

The Buddha pinpoints that it is the *carelessness* of mind and body, as a result of taking drugs and alcohol, that causes errors in our thinking and behaviour.

This carelessness is avoided if the cause, the drug itself, is given up and avoided.

How does the type of carelessness that results from drug taking work.

Drugs dominate a man's mind and body. This causes him to lose the power of sane and rational judgement, of vigilance.

As a result of this, he makes mistakes.

In this context, it is worth noting that intoxicants that cause carelessness don't only enter the body directly through the mouth or nose as 'drugs' that grow as plants in the earth or come out of a chemist's laboratory as pills.

They can enter through the eye or ear first by catching the attention of the outward-looking mind.

Physical carelessness is preceded by mental carelessness.

Mental carelessness is provoked through the eyes by reading, watching TV and using computers; and through the ears, by hearing or listening to unwholesome language, speech and propaganda.

You can become addicted to gambling, watching horror films and bullfights, hunting, shooting and fishing, overeating.

Or even your mobile phone?

> *"Phone addiction hurts our brains,"* reports The New York Times. *"Do you want to guess how many times you pull out your smartphone each day? The number is startling.*
>
> *"The average person checks their phone 80 times per day, often to check those little red notifications on social media.*
>
> *"Our addiction to the rectangle in our pockets is having serious effects on our brain, from reducing our attention span to spiking our blood pressure and even diminishing our intelligence."*

Once the seeds of intoxication and carelessness germinate in the rich compost of desire in the mind, they set up chain reactions with the senses. Each feeds the other in its turn.

A recipe for disaster.

As an escape from reality, which is what drink and drug abuse is, books, entertainment and music are widely used. As any schoolboy knows.

And an escape from reality, whether the intoxication is primarily mental or physical or both, is the opposite of the Awakened One's path.

On the contrary, the aim of Buddhism is to see more of reality. To be vigilant and lift the veil and see everything more clearly for what it really is. Suffering. It is not hidden. It blazes brighter than the sun.

For us, the important thing is to start by applying cause and effect.

These things cause suffering to oneself and others. These things I will abstain from. No cause - no effect. No drink and drugs. No carelessness. No unguarded mind, no unwanted consequences.

The relationship between oneself and the world will be re-established in normality. The internal Path can now be trodden with a minimum of external interference. With vigilance.

Appamādo amatapadaṃ
pamādo maccuno padaṃ
appamattā na mīyanti
ye pamattā yathā matā.

Vigilance is the state of deathlessness.
Negligence is the state of death.
The Vigilant do not die.
The Negligent are as if dead already.

Anything is possible.

NOTES

1. Awakened One. Buddha.

Buddho: means "awakened" in Pali/Sanskrit. It is the past participle of bodhati ("to wake"). Ultimately, it is from a Proto-Indo-European root meaning "to be awake, aware".

At no time, during the Buddha's lifetime was it used as a title with religious connotations as it is now. Just as, during his lifetime, there were no Buddha images or statues with people kneeling before them with their heads on the ground.

So *Buddho* just describes someone who has woken up.

Anyone. In any time or place.

Siddhartha never called himself *The Buddha*. He consistently referred to himself as "Tathāgata" "one who has thus gone". Simply put he was saying, if you do (go) exactly as I do (thus), you will end up awake just like me, in the same place (i.e. Nibbāna).

"Ehipassiko!" Come and see! (Wake up!)

2. This is the Third Precept:

**Kāmesumicchācārā veramanī
sikkhāpadam samādiyāmi.**

I undertake to refrain from misuse of the senses.

Kāmesumicchācārā, literally and originally, means: *misuse of the senses.* That is, any of the senses.

Later, it acquired the more limited meaning of sexual misconduct.

This is variously interpreted by different cultures and in different places. Misleadingly, it has acquired the status of a standard English translation.

Of course, it can include adultery and paedophilia.

But it is not only misuse of sexual desire.

It is misuse of <u>any</u> senses contacting their sense objects and setting up a state of interactive pollution with the mind.

Think of those Roman gluttons who, having eaten as much as they could, vomited it all up and returned for more!

Think of youngsters with earphones on full blast to shut out the world.

Think of Cleopatra and her vials of perfume and daily baths in fresh asses' milk.

Think of drunkenness, drug addiction, body piercing, masochism. Think of uncontrolled thinking.

THE QUIET MIND

The sun
shines
in a bucket of water
but doesn't
get
wet.

www.ingramcontent.com/pod-product-compliance
Lightning Source LLC
Chambersburg PA
CBHW020448030426
42337CB00014B/1452